D0605916

SEVEN WONDERS of the SOLAR SYSTEM

DAVID A. AGUILAR

This book is dedicated to Chesley Bonestell, who graciously spent many a sunny afternoon with me sharing his visions of art, space exploration, Hollywood sci-fi movies, and life as an artist who survived the Great San Francisco Earthquake of 1906. It is also dedicated to the cleverly inventive Ms. Astrid, my ingenious editor Sheila Keenan, and expressive art director Jim Hoover. Most of all, it is dedicated to all you young space dreamers out there. It's your turn to go forth and conquer the solar system!

— D.A.

This book also would not have been possible without enlightened input from Dr. Alan Stern, Dr. Owen Gingerich, Dr. James R. Zimbelman, and Ira Flatow.

VIKING
An imprint of Penguin Random House LLC
375 Hudson Street
New York, New York 10014

First published in the United States of America by Viking,
an imprint of Penguin Random House LLC, 2017

LIBRARY OF CONGRESS CATALOGING-IN-PUBLICATION DATA IS AVAILABLE
ISBN: 9780451476852

Manufactured in China Set in Legacy and Classic Robot

10 9 8 7 6 5 4 3 2 1

CONTENTS

Introduction 4
Mars 13
Europa 21
Saturn's Rings 29
Titan 37
Pluto & Charon 45
Planet Nine 52
Earth & Moon 61
Into the Future 69
Other Wonders 70
Dreams of Outer Space 72
In the Studio with David A. Aguilar 74
Keep Exploring! 78
Index 79

INTRODUCTION

THE SEVEN WONDERS of the Ancient World were magnificent architectural structures built thousands of years ago in countries bordering the Mediterranean Sea. There were many "wonders" lists circulated by different Greek authors; these lists were more tourist guides than historical documents. The Seven Wonders were classified as *theamata*, a Greek word meaning "things that must be seen." These marvelous examples of human achievement included the Great Pyramid of Giza, the Hanging Gardens of Babylon, the Temple of Artemis, the statue of Zeus at Olympia, the Mausoleum at Halicarnassus, the Colossus of Rhodes, and the Lighthouse at Alexandria.

Today, the Great Pyramid of Giza is the only one of the original seven wonders that remains. The pyramid of Khufu, as the Egyptians call it, covers more than thirteen acres, is constructed from more than two million stone blocks weighing between two and thirty-two tons each, and is one of the largest pyramids ever built. Believed to have been finished in 2560 BCE, the pyramid of Khufu remained the tallest structure on Earth for the next 4,000 years.

Over time, the other six wonders fell into ruin and disappeared. A series of earthquakes felled the Lighthouse at Alexandria, built to guide ships to safe harbor in northern Egypt. The incredible Hanging Gardens of Babylon may have been more legend than reality; the 40-foot-tall (12 m) golden statue of Zeus in Olympia was destroyed by fire. The Temple of Artemis in Turkey crumbled before invading armies. The Mausoleum at Halicarnassus was shaken to the ground by earthquakes, and the 100-foot (30 m) statue the Colossus of Rhodes collapsed during yet another earthquake, and later was recycled as scrap metal by invading Arab armies. (The Colossus was an inspiration for the Statue of Liberty in New York City's harbor.)

We still look to these Seven Wonders as celebrations of human achievement. But other wonders exist beyond those produced by Earth's great civilizations . . . *way* beyond. Humans had no hand in making these wonders, but nature did. May I present you with *The Seven Wonders of the Solar System*!

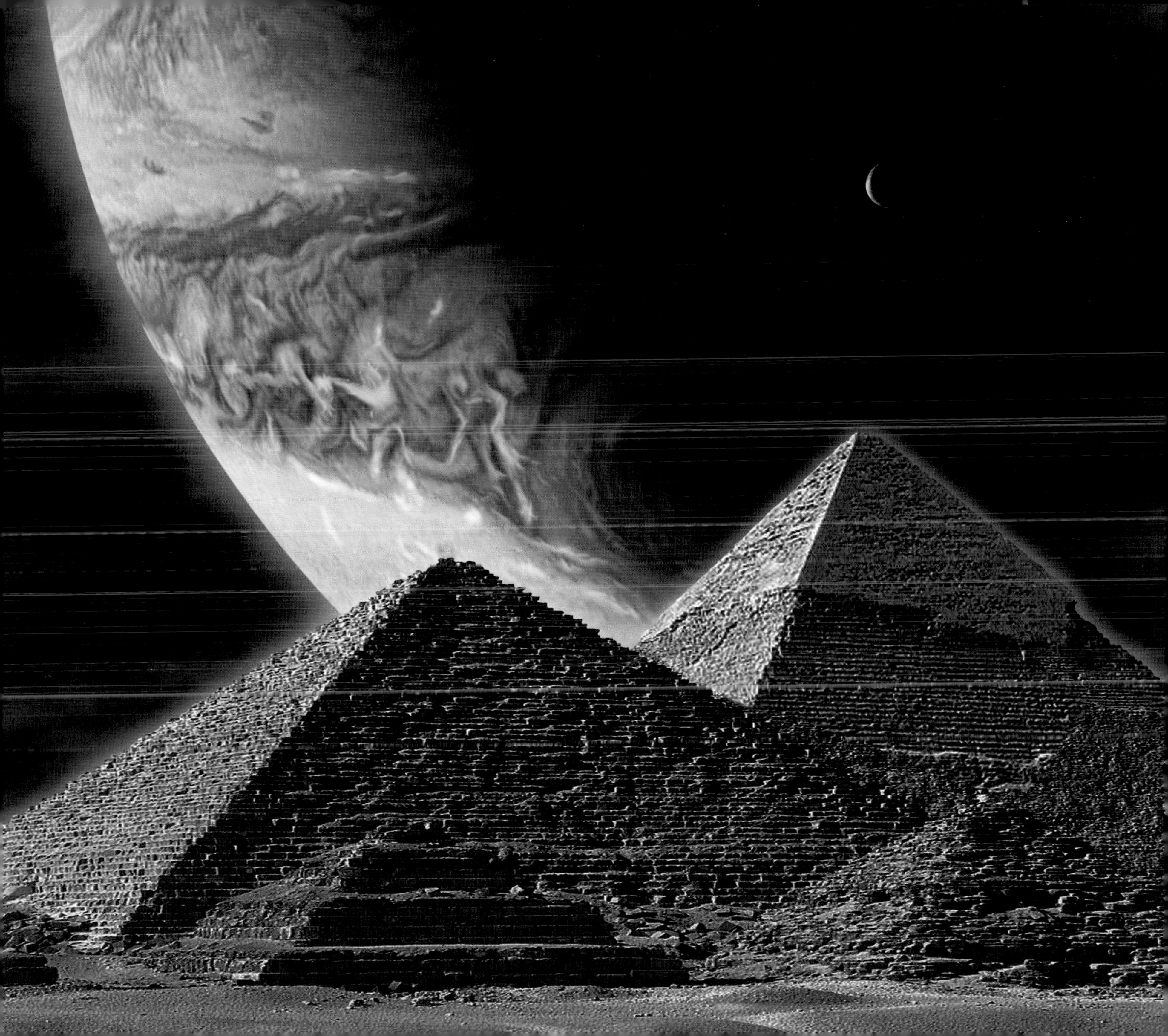

Like most of the Seven Ancient Wonders, the earliest traces of the formation of Earth and the solar system have vanished. However, there is a way to find out about the origins of our sun, the planets and their moons, comets, and other celestial objects. Astronomers looking into space see new solar systems forming everywhere. By studying these new beginnings, we can witness the same planet-forming processes that created our own sun and planets, and that's exciting!

Earth's story began about 4.6 billion years ago when a small cloud of gas and dust drifting through space was hit by a shockwave from a nearby supernova. This caused the cloud to compress and collapse down into a spinning disk. In the center, where most of the material was concentrated, temperatures became so hot, hydrogen atoms joined together to form helium atoms, resulting in nuclear fusion. Gobbling up 99.8 percent of all the gas and dust available in the disk, a new shining star was born. We call it the sun. The remaining 0.2 percent of stellar material became the planets, moons, asteroids, and comets. Planets closest to the hot sun—Mercury, Venus, Earth, and Mars—were made of rock. Farther out, colossal amounts of gas and ice not boiled away by the searing heat generated by the sun joined together and formed Jupiter, Saturn, Uranus, and Neptune. At the furthest reaches of our solar system, dwarf planets, comets, and asteroids remained as the leftover building blocks of the early solar neighborhood.

Compared to other stars in space, our glorious, life-sustaining sun is a medium-sized, middle-aged, gold-colored gem that has enough fuel to shine for another five billion years. Because the sun is so large, nearly 1 million miles (1.5 million km) in diameter, the force of its powerful gravity keeps all the planets from flying away into space. It's like a giant magnet that holds our solar system together.

Planets in our solar system are like people! They come in all colors, sizes, weights, and densities. Venus appears bright white due to a thick layer of clouds that blots out its surface and brilliantly reflects sunlight. White-hot Venus is almost 8,000 miles (12,800 km) in diameter and as dense as a rock. Striped Jupiter soars in at 89,000 miles (143,000 km) in diameter with a natural creamy color and bands of brown and red stripes. Amazingly, Jupiter is only about as dense as a Nerf ball!

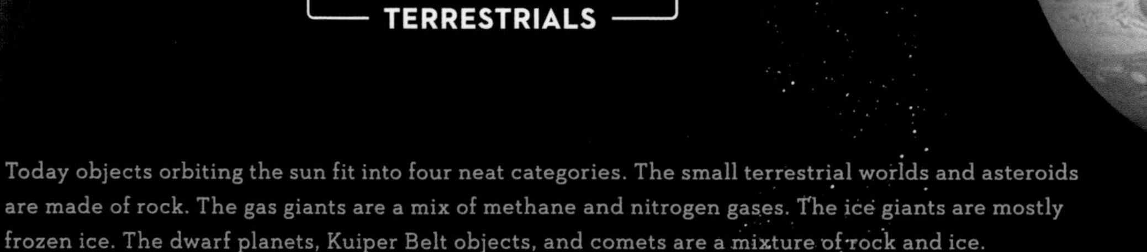

Today objects orbiting the sun fit into four neat categories. The small terrestrial worlds and asteroids are made of rock. The gas giants are a mix of methane and nitrogen gases. The ice giants are mostly frozen ice. The dwarf planets, Kuiper Belt objects, and comets are a mixture of rock and ice.

For thousands of years, the only method used to study the planets was to watch and record their movements across the heavens. To the Greeks, the planets were not spherical orbs, they were gods traveling back and forth across the sky to visit different "houses" or what we call the zodiac constellations. Many people today think it's funny if you ask, "What's your sign?" but they didn't in the ancient world! Astrologers carefully tracked the motions of the planets to cast fortunes or predict future events.

With the invention of astronomical instruments, the study of astrology turned into the science of astronomy. But observers could still be fooled. At times Venus's orbit around the sun caused it to appear in the morning sky just before sunrise. Then, months later, Venus showed up in the evening sky at sunset! Ancient people thought they were seeing two separate objects, so they named one the evening star and the other the morning star. In reality, both turned out to be tricky Venus.

Telescopes brought the planets closer into view. Now we could see the illustrious polar ice caps on

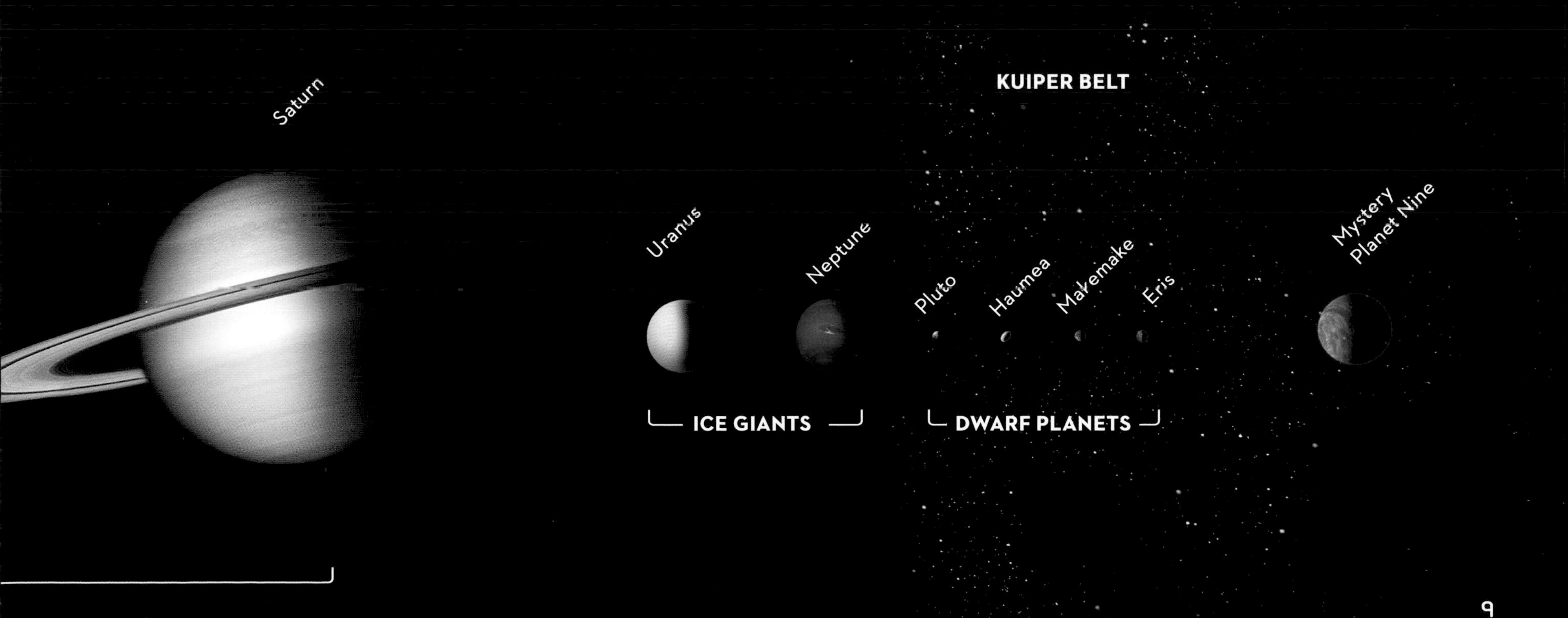

Mars, the bands in the atmosphere of Jupiter, and the curious rings circling Saturn. Telescopes enabled us to identify planets previously invisible to the unaided eye. Still, when we studied the planets telescopically, Earth's atmosphere often got in the way. Winds and turbulence made planets appear to waver in and out of focus. Even photographs taken from mountaintops could be fuzzy. Many decades would pass before new technologies made it possible to send spacecraft directly to the planets. Then robotic explorers could investigate distant worlds up close and even land on their surfaces.

Today's robotic probes have visited every major planet as well as two dwarf planets: Ceres in the asteroid belt and Pluto in the Kuiper Belt. Most recently a robot explorer landed on a speeding comet during its orbit around the sun. This was almost unthinkable a few decades ago! Although no human has ever set foot on another planet beyond Earth, robotic explorers are doing the job for us, revealing a vast number of new discoveries in our planetary neighborhood. When will humans be able to journey to the edge of our solar system? It may happen before the end of the twenty-first century but why wait until then? Using the latest scientific data and spacecraft images, we can blast off on an imaginary journey to explore these distant worlds as if we were actually there. Our trip begins now.

MARS

IF YOU ROCKET out to Mars, the fourth planet from the sun, the eerie pink sky may make you wish you were back on Earth—but that's 34 million miles (54 million km) away at its closest approach to Mars. Ancient sky watchers marveled at Mars's odd iron-red appearance. They saw power and wrath in the planet's redness, characteristics they believed it shared with mighty Mars, the Roman god of war.

Mars is a terrestrial planet about half the size of Earth. Its atmosphere is 100 times less dense than ours, and the abundant iron oxide on its surface generates a perpetual rusty glow. The Martian atmosphere contains high levels of carbon dioxide, making it impossible for non-Martians like us to breathe. Although this atmosphere is quite thin, it does contain wispy clouds, gentle breezes, and erratic dust storms. And get this: it never rains here . . . but it snows! On Mars, when fluffy snowflakes fall to the ground, they're made mostly of frozen carbon dioxide, occasionally with some water ice mixed in.

The atmosphere of Mars lacks the insulating properties necessary to retain thermal energy. Heat absorbed from the sun in daytime radiates right back out into space at night. On a warm Martian day,

temperatures around the planet's equator can reach a balmy 70 degrees F (21 degrees C). As the evening sets in, nighttime temperatures at the same location quickly plunge to a chilling -100 degrees F (-73 degrees C).

On Mars there are no oceans or rivers or lakes, at least not anymore. Today Mars is a planet-wide desert covered with boulders ejected from ancient meteorite craters. However, here we encounter the first wonder of our imaginary journey. What is this strange monster mountain standing before us? It's the magnificent Olympus Mons, the largest volcano in the solar system.

Volcanoes originate as vents or cracks in a planet's crust where molten lava, ash, and gas force their way up to the surface. The visible cone that increasingly swells upward is what we recognize as the volcano. On Earth there are four different types of volcanoes: cinder cones, stratovolcanoes, shields, and lava domes. On Mars we find shield volcanoes that are enormous, gently sloping mountains built up by slowly spreading flows of molten lava. Their smooth outlines resemble turtle shells or a medieval armored knight's shield.

Located on the Tharsis Montes plains near the equator of Mars, Olympus Mons is one of a dozen large shield volcanoes found here. Compared to Olympus Mons, Earth's largest volcano, Mauna Loa (55,770 feet [17,000 m] from ocean floor base to summit), and Mt. Everest (29, 029 feet [8,848 m]) are mere lumps on the ground. Rising 16 miles (27 km)—that would be 84,840 feet (25,859 m)—above the Martian plateau, Olympus Mons is breathtaking to see. It is so big that if you stood on the surface of Olympus Mons, you could not see it as a mountain; both the top and the bottom would be hidden by the curved horizon of Mars.

After free climbing the 600-foot-high (182 m) cliffs at the base of Olympus Mons, you could ride a fat mountain bike to the extinct volcano's summit. Cruising along on the gentle five degree slope, you would need to cover 50 miles (80 km) of volcanic terrain before reaching the top. The view would be spectacular! You'd be at an altitude that's twice as high as airplanes fly on Earth, from which you could see the top of the Martian atmosphere and the visible curvature of the planet. "Awesome" doesn't begin to cover this planetary bike ride. Oh, there's one small detail before you shred it to the top: make sure you bring along enough oxygen to make this 100-mile (160 km) round-trip.

At the summit of Olympus Mons, you will encounter its caldera, the opening through which lava flowed 3.5 billion years ago. This caldera is 53 miles (85 km) in diameter; that's larger than the distance across Rhode Island! Hiking down to the caldera's center, you would see a gigantic hole with ringed cliffs

Wispy Martian clouds swirl around the base of Olympus Mons, the largest volcano in the solar system.

rising six miles (9.5 km) high all around it. Makes you wonder: how did this Martian volcano get so big?

On Earth, the continents we live on float on top of the hot molten magma located miles beneath them. We call this phenomenon plate tectonics. Over millions of years, these tectonic plates shift and move around over the surface of our planet. This movement prevents large buildups of lava on the surface, which therefore limits the size of our volcanoes. On Mars, there are no plate tectonics or separate continents moving around. Once lava begins welling up deep inside the planet, the lava flow that reaches the surface doesn't stop. Over time—again, we're talking a *long* time—the volcano grows larger and larger, eventually dwarfing everything around it.

Today the surface of Mars bears the scars of an ancient geologic past. Magnificent canyons slash across its landscape, which is also crisscrossed by dry riverbeds where water once flowed billions of years ago. Mars is a vast red desert terrain unlike any other place in the solar system. So how did Olympus Mons and the other surrounding volcanoes on the Tharsis plateau change and affect the history of this planet?

Billions of years ago, as lava flowed down the sides of these volcanoes like rust-tinged honey, volcanic gases composed of carbon dioxide, methane, and water filled the atmosphere, temporarily heating the planet by trapping the energy from the sun. Similar to today's accumulation of greenhouse gases in our atmosphere, molecules of carbon dioxide caused Mars to warm up. Giant Martian polar ice caps melted into rivers that flowed into rising seas. Clouds formed, winds blew, and rains fell from the skies pierced by lightning bolts. It was a hot mess! Fiery rivers of lava from Olympus Mons and surrounding volcanoes became so dense that billions of tons of lava churned out over an area 3,100 miles (5,000 km) wide, forming a lava layer 7.5 miles (12 km) thick. Mars became so lopsided from flowing lava that it tilted more than 23 degrees on its axis. For comparison, if this same shift happened here on Earth, Paris would end up in the northern polar circle. The "city of light" would become "the city of auroras."

After millions of years of extreme activity, Olympus Mons and the nearby volcanoes stopped erupting. The magma beneath them cooled. The smoke and steam drifted away and their calderas and volcanic openings cooled and solidified. With no more steam coming out of volcanoes, clouds disappeared, and it stopped raining. Rivers stopped flowing, and the planet's oceans slowly evaporated into space. Mars became the dead, silent, cold world we explore today.

Considering its present condition, why do we even bother to send spacecraft to Mars? It's nearby, and that's a big plus! But two other bodies are closer to Earth: the moon and Venus. However, unlike Mars, our moon has no atmosphere to protect us from harmful cosmic rays and destructive solar radiation. Food will not grow in its soil. Planetary hotspot Venus has surface temperatures that can melt lead. Toxic sulfuric acid rains down from the skies, and the crushing atmospheric pressure on its surface equals that found 3,000 feet (900 m) underwater on Earth. There's absolutely no fun to be had on Venus!

In comparison, Mars is a bit more hospitable. There are no rainstorms, hurricanes, floods, or "Mars quakes" to shake things up. (Though extreme dust storms can be so strong they blot out the surface features of the planet for months at a time.)

The soil on Mars contains water we can extract for drinking and irrigating plants inside future greenhouses. Using chemical devices, we can separate Martian water into oxygen to breathe and hydrogen to burn as fuel. Mars may be cold at night, but it is still temperate enough for us to survive. There is

ample sunlight to grow food and power solar panels for electricity. Gravity is one-third of Earth's, but astronauts can adjust and easily move around. The thin Martian atmosphere allows some necessary protection from cosmic and solar radiation, but permanent houses could be built underground to provide better shielding. Bonus! The length of days and nights are nearly the same as those on Earth. We know that in the foreseeable future, humans will not be able to walk on the surface of Mars without wearing a spacesuit. They will not be able to breathe in the Martian air or feel fresh breezes or the warmth of sunlight on their faces. Even though the moon or Venus may be closer, human exploration of Mars is on! Many nations, including the United States, believe they can send the first humans to Mars in the 2030s. When astronauts get there, they'll see Olympus Mons from up to 100 miles (160 km) away from anywhere on the Martian surface. The tallest mountain and largest volcano in the solar system will be a very clear reminder of a period of time when Mars was a different world. Surrounded by seas, flowing rivers, meandering streams, and possibly real Martian life-forms, Olympus Mons and the other Tharsis volcanoes are like the great Egyptian pyramids on Earth. They are magnificent structures that have survived the ravages of time. They truly are mystical wonders to behold.

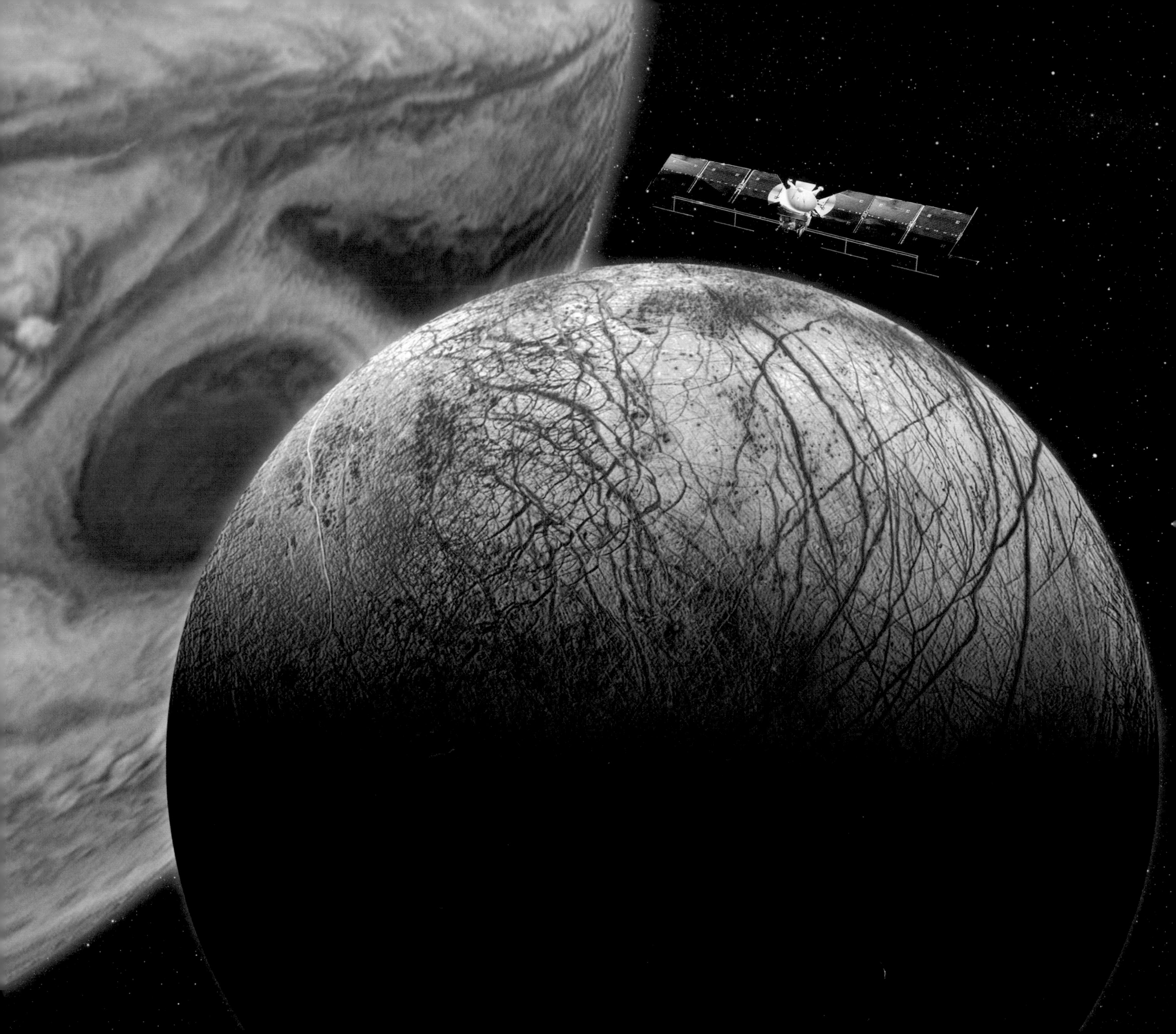

EUROPA

WE LIVE ON a planet where 70 percent of the surface is covered by deep blue oceans. From space, puffy white clouds float above this surface, with hints of tan and emerald-green continents peeking through from below. Is Earth the only water world in our solar system?

Evidence tells us Mars once supported vast oceans with killer tsunami waves that rushed across them. Today all we see are barren riverbeds and dried-up sea bottoms. Those bodies of water disappeared billions of years ago. Venus, our overheated neighbor, may once have had oceans with waves crashing on rocky shores, but those also evaporated long ago. Today, we are still not certain how the oceans on Earth originated. Did steam venting from vast volcanoes condense into clouds, causing rain to fill up the rocky basins with immense amounts of water? Or did asteroids and comets crashing into our world bring new water with them to share on our primordial planet?

New research shows that Earth's oceans may be almost as old as the Earth itself. That would be about 4.5 billion years old (though it doesn't look a day over 4.4999 billion years!). Water and life on our planet are closely connected. Sometimes, we may take our abundance of water for granted without considering why water is so important to life. For one thing, water dissolves just about everything found in nature, even the precious metal gold. (Did you know that all seawater contains traces of dissolved gold?) Water is the best known solvent in the universe. All living

organisms use water to transport dissolved chemicals and nutrients from cell to cell. Our own bodies are almost 65 percent liquid water!

Scientific evidence points to the first life on Earth perhaps beginning in the depths of our oceans, near black smoker vents that spewed out water heated by magma from below. This water is loaded with dissolved chemicals and minerals. Around these openings, warm nutrients and chains of molecules were exposed to conditions that spawned the first simple life-forms to inhabit Earth. When scientists search for signs of life on other planets, they say "follow the water." If you locate water, the probability is strong there may be life associated with it.

Picture an alien moon with an ocean that's deeper, darker, and larger than all Earth's oceans combined. Is there life swimming in these remote alien seas? To learn more, we'll need to travel way beyond the asteroid belt to the fifth planet in our solar system, the gas giant Jupiter. Here we encounter Europa, the second wonder of our journey through the solar system. The oceans we're seeking lie hidden beneath a thick shell of surface ice on the moon Europa.

Europa is one of four large moons orbiting Jupiter. The Italian astronomer Galileo Galilei discovered it just over four centuries ago when he pointed his handmade telescope toward Jupiter one evening in 1610. He saw the round gas giant surrounded by four little dots that changed their positions as they orbited Jupiter.

Roughly the size of our own moon, Europa is immersed in strong radiation fields generated by humongo Jupiter. On the icy, cracked surface of Europa, life exposed for any length of time would be "zapped" into dust. But hidden underneath the miles-thick ice, where radiation does not penetrate, conditions for life become much more promising. Here, in Europa's darkened global ocean, warm liquid saltwater bathes the entire moon, plunging to the extreme depth of 60 miles (97 km).

How do we know this ocean is saltwater? Astronomers studying the icy landscape have detected salt crystals lying on the surface that were deposited through deep cracks in the ice. These salts were dissolved from rocks eroded by water over many millions of years, just like the process that created the salty oceans on Earth.

Since Europa is so far away from the heat of the sun, why haven't its waters turned into solid ice over all these billions of years? Europa does not have a molten core like the Earth to heat its oceans. Instead, like two kids pulling on either end of a rope, Jupiter and Europa are in a constant gravitational tug-of-war. Jupiter pulls on Europa, and it pulls back, with neither one yielding to the other. To make things even more difficult, gravitational fields generated by Jupiter's other moons

Jupiter and four of its moons (left to right): Io, Europa, Ganymede, and Callisto.

Europa has more water than Earth. The average depth of Europa's ocean is 60 miles (97 km). The average depth of Earth's oceans is only about 12,000 feet (3,700 m).

Ganymede and Io also pull on Europa, causing large tidal fluctuations that produce huge amounts of internal heat. This is why Europa's oceans remain liquid and do not freeze. Not surprisingly, with all this tugging going on, the surface of Europa exhibits large cracks, some of which are 12 miles (19 km) wide. These sienna-colored scars are created when surface ices twist and shatter, drawing ocean water from below to the surface, where it quickly freezes.

On Earth, the deepest part of our oceans is an underwater valley called the Challenger Deep, which is located in the western Pacific's Marianas Trench. This valley plunges 6.8 miles (11 km) down into perpetual darkness. Compare this to Europa's colossally deep ocean and something startling is revealed. (No, it's not the birthplace of Godzilla!) On a moon one-fourth the size of Earth, there is double the amount of water. When it comes to ocean worlds in our solar system, Europa reigns number one! This presents an intriguing question. How can a moon so small have more water on it than Earth? The answer is the depth of the ocean. Europa's waters are nine times deeper than the oceans of Earth.

What might life be like in such a deep ocean?

It would be life adapted to complete darkness. With a layer of ice at least one mile (1.6 km) thick above its liquid waters, very little diffused light would penetrate Europa's deep waters. Say hello to infinite nighttime. Creatures on this distant moon might be found clustered around deep thermal vents on the ocean's floor or swimming freely about. Some might make their own light like glow sticks to attract prey or frighten menacing predators. Europan life might camp upside down on the underside of the ice sheets, much like the creatures we find in the hidden waters of Antarctica. Other evidence points to the existence of lakes completely encased in ice separated from the main ocean. This might present an entirely different type of habitat, one that receives some sunlight from our distant sun plus added sunlight reflected off Jupiter. One day we may be able to drill down, down, down through Europa's ice crust and launch a robotic probe to explore these alien waters. The incredible technology necessary for success is being developed today. It's quite possible we'll find that the largest ocean in the solar system may hold life stranger than we have ever known on Earth.

Unlike Earth's moon, the surface of Europa is covered entirely in ice, without any large craters or

Hidden beneath an icy surface, alien life capable of creating its own light may shine brightly in Europa's dark ocean.

tall mountains. This tells us the surface is young and active. The daily rise and fall of Europa's surface, caused by the constant pull of Jupiter and the other large moons, evens out the landscape. Standing on this moon, we would see cracks and ridges only a few meters high. Astronauts walking Europa's surface would have to be diligent. Jupiter is surrounded by intense radiation belts that bombard the inner moons; surface explorers would have to wear heavily protected spacesuits. The best place for humans to land or set up camp would be at the leading edge of Europa as it orbits Jupiter. Here the radiation is much weaker. Looking out, spectacular Jupiter would fill an area of the sky 24 times larger than our own moon appears at home.

While moonwalking Europa, you would experience ice quakes and occasionally giant plumes of snow shooting out of fresh cracks in the ground. Gravity here is only 13 percent of Earth's, so you could easily cover great distances hopping like a kangaroo. More good news: a day on Europa equals 3.5 Earth days, so summer vacation would be three and a half times longer! Sadly, there would be no winds, clouds, or color to the pitch-black sky. Smoky-gray Ganymede, Jupiter's largest moon, would rise and set every two days, appearing 1.5 times larger than our moon. Because it is so much closer, the yellow-and-orange-colored moon Io would appear a bit larger than farther away Ganymede, rising and setting twice each day. If you were standing on the frozen crust of this distant moon, Earth would shine like a tiny blue-tinted diamond in the sky. You would be gazing back at our distant water world teeming with life, from another world with an ocean grander than Earth's five oceans and seven seas combined.

SATURN'S RINGS

EARTH'S SURFACE RADIATES with majestic blue oceans. Luminous Venus bounces the sun's blinding light back into space and shape-shifts in phases just like our moon. As winter approaches, rusty Mars struts two gleaming polar ice caps while giant dust devils twist across its barren red deserts. Two horizontal red stripes and a giant red spot dominate Jupiter's windswept, cloud-covered face. And Saturn's beautiful planetary ring system graces our solar system like no other.

The sixth planet from the sun, Saturn is a gas giant like Jupiter, although smaller: approximately 74,901 miles (120,536 km) in diameter versus Jupiter's 86,881 miles (139,822 km). Saturn spins so quickly on its axis that a day lasts just 10.5 hours. This rapid rotation causes its planetary middle to bulge 7,500

miles (12,000 km) outward, making Saturn the most "irregular" or oval-shaped planet in our solar system. Whirling around this butterscotch-hued world are billions of tons of sparkling ice and rock that form at least eight distinct rings combined into one beautiful system so bright, so wide, it resembles a glittering circular racetrack. If these chunks of ice were race cars, they would be flying along in thousands of different lanes, hurtling along at different speeds with tiny herder moons following along like speeding police cars weaving in and out of the lanes.

At 599,181 miles (964,288 km) in diameter, Saturn's brighter visible rings can be subdivided into more than eight separate sections: three main rings, five dusty smaller rings, and one dark ring. Astronomers named each ring using letters of the alphabet. The A and B rings are separated by a dark gap in the rings called the Cassini Division, named for the Italian astronomer who discovered it in 1675. On a clear night, you can easily see all three of the main rings with a small telescope. Viewed separately, there are A, B, C, D, E, F, and G rings, but the order is different going out from the planet because the letter names were applied as new divisions were detected using better telescopes. Packed together, the rings of Saturn are so substantial it would take 45 days to fly all the way around the outer F ring in an airliner.

The largest planets in our solar system, Jupiter, Saturn, Uranus, and Neptune, were the first to form. Composed mostly of hydrogen and helium gas, they accumulated early building materials long before the original solar nebula disappeared. As our solar system formed, the gas giants came together

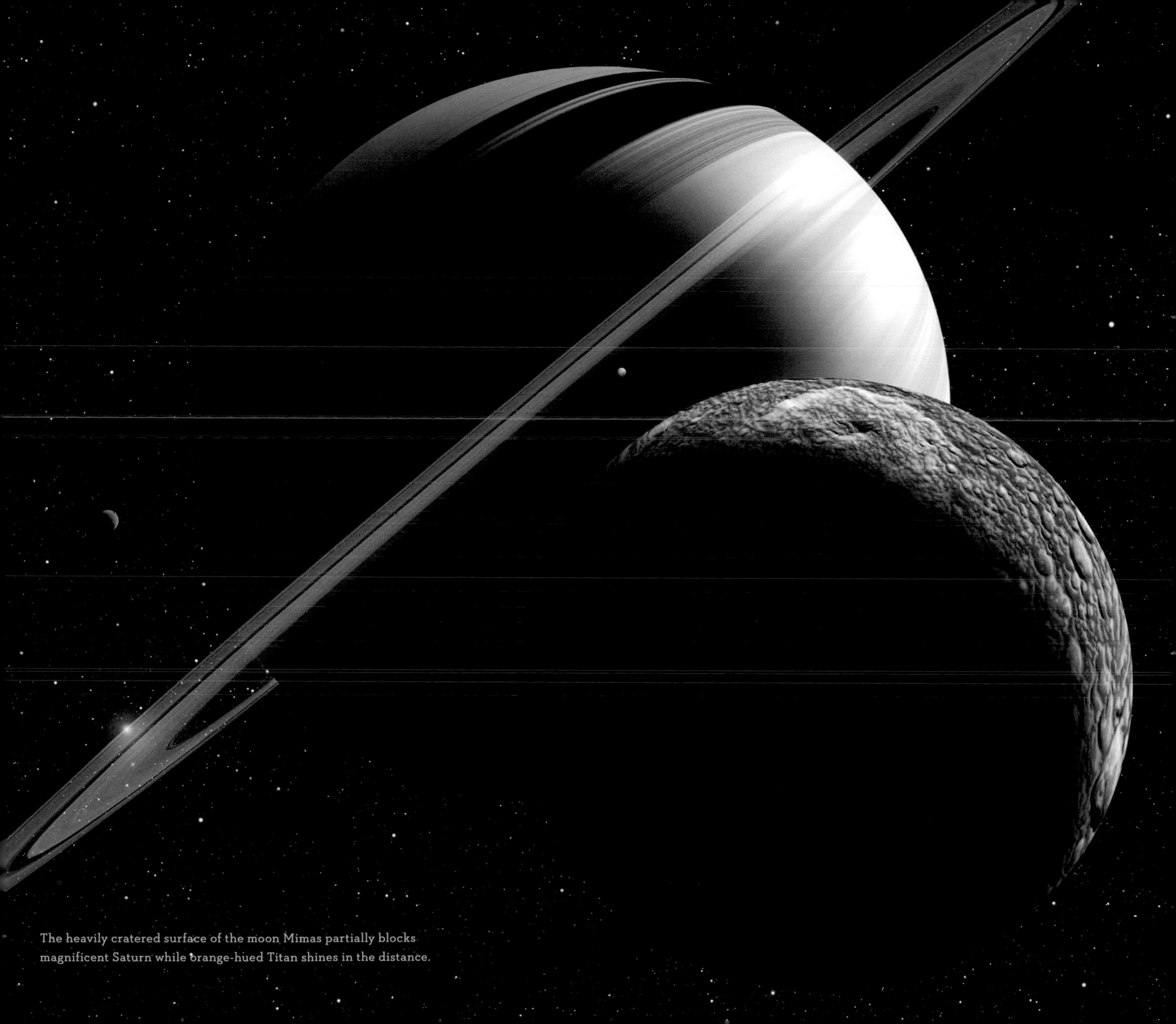

The heavily cratered surface of the moon Mimas partially blocks magnificent Saturn while orange-hued Titan shines in the distance.

quickly and developed within 1 to 10 million years. Earth, Venus, Mercury, and Mars took longer to emerge. Made mostly of rock and very few gases, they evolved over a period of 30 to 100 million years. Not only are the gas giant planets older than the rocky planets, they have an extra bonus the rocky planets do not have. All of the gas and ice giant worlds have rings. Yet none compare in size or sheer dazzle to Saturn's rings. Therein lies the mystery! Where did Saturn get its large rings?

One hypothesis, or working idea, is that the rings developed out of the orbiting ice and dust left over after Saturn formed. Pushed and prodded by Saturn's gravitational field, these random particles of ice and dust flattened out into the magnificent ring structure we see today. A more recent hypothesis points to an accidental collision between a massive comet and an orbiting moon, or between two small moons, that spread out to form the rings.

Saturn's extensive ring system is composed mostly of plain old chunks of ice ranging in size from a grain of salt to tumbling icebergs. The physical size of the rings is staggering. The measured diameter to the outer edge of the narrow F ring is 174,257 miles (280,440 km)! That's very, very large. In a different perspective, it would take almost twenty-one Earths lined up side by side to span the entire diameter of the rings. Surprisingly, the thickness of the rings varies, with some as thin as 30 feet (10 m), and others as thick as half a mile (0.3 km). This makes them disappear when viewed on edge. No wonder astronomers shook their heads in disbelief when the rings did their vanishing act!

Now let's imagine going back in time to a stone-walled courtyard in Tuscany, Italy, with a swiftly moving stream running below. The year is 1610 and we've time-traveled to one of the most prestigious universities in the world, the University of Padua. On this early January evening, a man standing next to a rock wall steadies himself as he holds a long narrow tube in his hands. One end of the tube is almost touching his eye while the other is pointed at a bright-looking pale yellow-colored star in the sky. At this moment, he is about to become the first person to ever see Saturn and its rings. Gazing through his primitive 25-power telescope, Galileo Galilei squinted, probably wiped the lenses clean on his tunic, and observed again because apparently to his eyes, Saturn had "ears." Galileo was unable to clearly see the rings. To him, Saturn looked like a tiny cream-colored sphere with mouse ears on each side. Now a new mystery was about to unfold. Over the coming years, those "ears" would disappear, completely fading away as if they never existed. Then, after a period of time, they would return again. Forty-five years later, using a more powerful telescope mounted in the front yard of the Paris Observatory in France, Dutch astronomer Christiaan Huygens clearly observed Saturn and concluded that it was indeed a world surrounded by a ring so thin that it disappeared when viewed edge on.

On October 15, 1997, an unmanned robotic spacecraft named Cassini was launched; it traveled through space for seven years before arriving at Saturn in 2004. Cassini's top mission was to map the 3-D structure of the rings. In 2005, the spacecraft flew behind the rings and transmitted radio signals through them back toward Earth. This is how we learned the rings were not uniform in thickness.

Composed primarily of hydrogen and helium gases with some ammonia ices and water mixed in, Saturn has a very low density. A Styrofoam ball is low in density. It's soft and lightweight: you can poke holes in it with your finger. A steel ball the same size has much more density to it. The atoms in steel are packed closer together than they are in Styrofoam. This makes steel denser and heavier. Just try sticking your finger into a steel ball; it's not going to work! Saturn, the lightest world with the least density of all the planets in the solar system, presents some interesting possibilities. If you found a lake large enough and dropped big old Saturn and its rings into it, it would float like a cork. It would remain bobbing up and down like a big boat. Earth, on the other hand, is mostly made out of rock, and if we tried this same experiment, it would sink like a ton of cement. So long, little rocky world!

Since other planets have rings, too, how do they compare to Saturn's? Jupiter has three ghostly dust rings named the outer gossamer rings and the inner halo ring. Uranus has thirteen faint rings that resemble circles of string. Neptune has three main rings that are not the same thickness all around. Two have bulges in the middle, like a snake that just ate a rodent. One question we have not asked about these wonders is how long they will last. Saturn's rings may have been around since the formation of the solar system 4.5 billion years ago, or they may have formed a bit later. Today it appears they are quite stable and will be around many more billions of years. They aren't going anywhere.

Earth

TITAN

SATURN NOT only has gorgeous rings surrounding it, at least 60 moons are corralled around it, too. Can you imagine seeing 60 moons up in our night sky?

Titan, the largest and most intriguing moon of Saturn, is bigger than the planet Mercury. This satellite may be a celestial knockout, but it's not a place you would like to call home. On its warmest summer days, high temperatures on Titan reach a glacial -290 degrees F (-180 degrees C) below zero!

This moon of Saturn is located nine and a half times farther from the sun than Earth is. Titan has an orange-colored atmosphere that is so thick it's like looking through the haze of a forest fire. The atmosphere is toxic, too. Okay, Titan does have lakes, rivers, streams, swamps, clouds, lightning, rain, and snow that make it seem Earth-like. But stop right there! Titan's lakes and seas are not filled with water. Water on this imposing moon remains frozen harder than rock. Liquids on this moon are made of organic gases like those that bubble up in murky swamps on Earth. With only faint warmth coming from the faraway sun, Titan's gases are so cold they have condensed into liquids. (Think propane fuel tanks used for barbecues. These tanks are filled with a gas that has been compressed until it has become a liquid. That's why the gas "sloshes" like water when you move the propane tank around.)

The name Titan comes from classical Greek literature. In Greek mythology, the Titans were a family of giant gods who were the first to rule Earth. They were the ancestors of Greek Olympian gods like Zeus, Hera, Poseidon, and Apollo.

Similar to that of our Earth and moon system, Titan's rotation is gravitationally bound to Saturn. This relationship is known as synchronous rotation; it means that the same side of Titan is always facing Saturn. The view from Titan gets tricky, too. Saturn's massiveness fills nearly half the sky, and it undergoes phase changes just like our own moon. Looming high above Titan, Saturn does not rise or set. Instead it morphs from a dark phase to a crescent, a half phase, a full phase, and then back to a dark phase—approximately every 15 days, 22 hours. During Saturn's dark phase, when the gas giant is situated between Titan and the sun, only its glowing rings, illuminated by the distant sun, are visible from Titan.

Curiously, Titan is considered to be the most Earth-like object in our solar system. Affirmative: it's a moon with an atmosphere in the coldest regions of space. What makes it so Earth-like?

If we travel back in time almost four billion years, Earth was blanketed with a rich organic methane atmosphere like Titan is today. During this early time period, our sun's energy output was 20 to 30 percent less than it is today. Earth should have been colder than it actually was during this formational time. Our organic atmospheric haze trapped precious heat and kept the Earth from freezing. It also shielded the first life on this planet from deadly ultraviolet solar radiation. Early Earth, like Titan today, would have been a challenging place for us to survive. The first creatures on Earth did not breathe oxygen. Oxygen was poison to them. They breathed methane air just like we find today on Titan. In time, single-celled oxygen-producing microbes blossomed in large numbers, converting the composition of Earth's atmosphere to what we breathe today. We know oxygen is essential for our bodies; it is used to change nutrients into powerful energy. Would there need to be more oxygen in Titan's atmosphere to support life there? Surprisingly, the answer is no.

There are life-forms here on Earth that carry on nicely without oxygen. They live around hot volcanic vents at the bottom of the oceans or buried in soil deep underground. They use methane instead of oxygen to convert food into energy. Some bacteria even consume methane and turn it back into oxygen. The surface of Titan may host abundant life fed by volcanoes that continuously burp out methane gas. So what type of life might that be?

If there is life on Titan, it probably would be very basic forms, like bacteria or single-celled protozoa. Here on Earth, living cells have outer membranes composed of fats that cover living cells like a wall. These membranes stop water-based fluids like your blood from mixing with outside fluids like the water from the ocean. Think about that one for a moment! Your cells have protective suits on. Titan's residents may also be made of cells with outside layers that keep them from freezing. Life on Titan—weird as it sounds—might contain a sort of cosmic antifreeze to protect it from turning into Popsicles.

Could larger, even more exotic life exist on this moon? It's possible, but probably not on the surface. Titan lacks a magnetic field to protect life from lethal solar radiation. It's likely this moon's surface is sparse when it comes to big things moving around on it. Hidden in the methane lakes and oceans, however, nightmarish creatures may exist beneath the ice in the alien seas. These life-forms might see their world differently, hear differently, and process their environment differently than we do. No matter: even if we discover that there's nothing more than single cells dog-paddling around in Titan's methane lakes, this fact

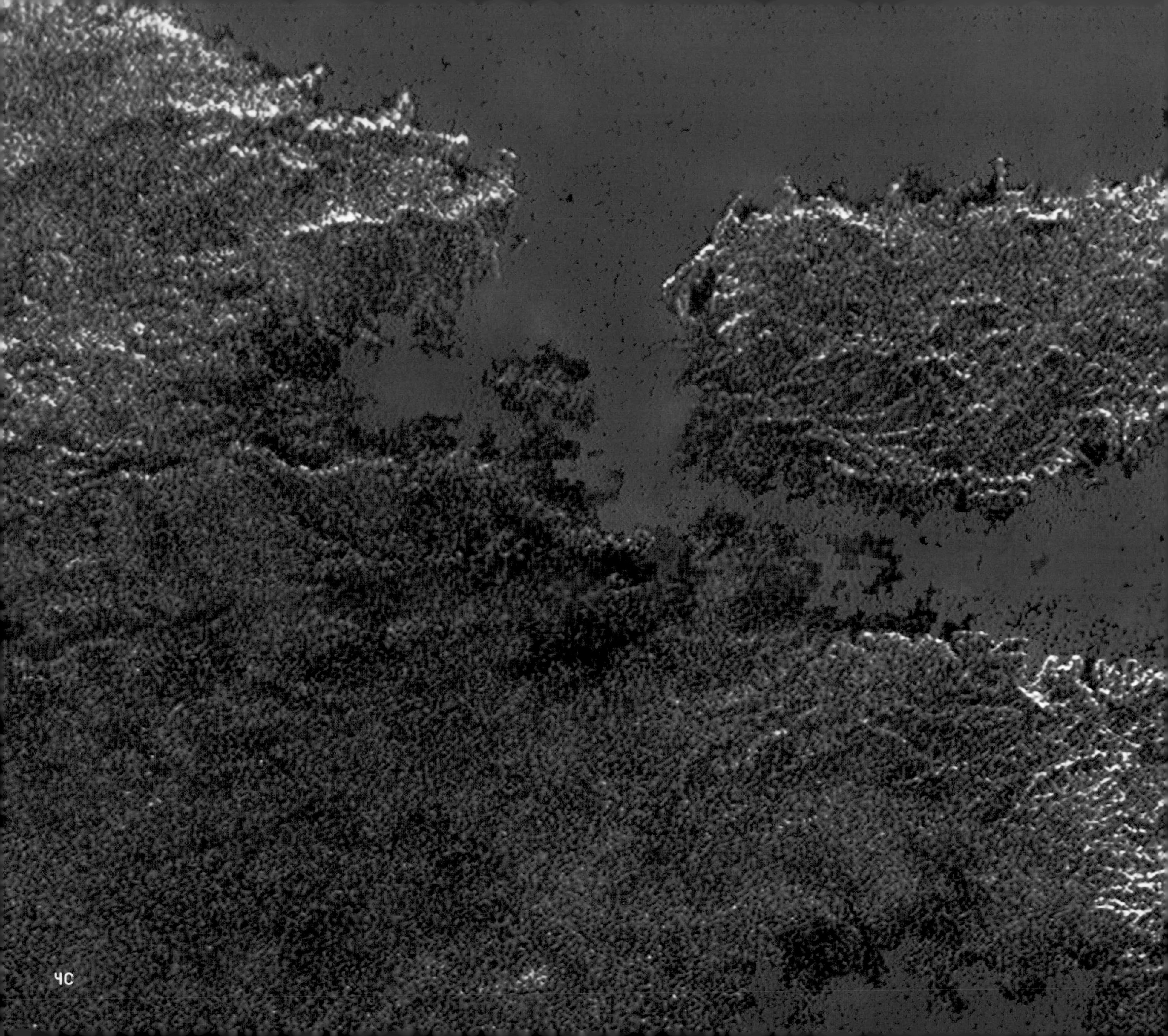
4C

alone could confirm the existence of other life in the universe.

OUR SKY IS BLUE. Mars has pink skies because of the red dust suspended in the air. Why is Titan's sky bright orange? When we break down its composition, we find that Titan's atmosphere is 97 percent nitrogen gas (ours is 79 percent nitrogen), and 3 percent methane, ethane, and carbon dioxide. The orange color comes from the rich abundance of organic molecules suspended in it.

Methane gas is corrosive. This means it can chemically eat away and dissolve seemingly indestructible things like rocks. For example, some of the famous Renaissance marble statues in Europe have suffered damage from the chemical hydrocarbons polluting the atmosphere. The statues are slowly being eaten away by them. On Titan, it's not the wind or rain that changes the landscape, it's the corrosive atmosphere that alters things. There are no tall mountains jutting up into the sky, no deep canyons cutting across the surface. The largest rock structures are only a few hundred meters high. Looking out over this eerie landscape, we'd see that the terrain gently rises and falls around smooth boulder formations. At the surface, the atmospheric pressure is about one and a half times that on Earth. Walking on Titan, you'd feel the same air pressure experienced when swimming 16 feet (4.8 m) underwater. Because this atmospheric pressure is substantial, no pressure suit is necessary to explore the surface. All you need is a breathing mask, really warm clothes, and a thin plastic covering to protect you from the corrosive methane rain.

One puzzling feature on Titan is the lack of waves on the lakes and oceans. On Earth, breezes far out at sea create huge waves that send surfers running for their surfboards. On Titan, the waters are flat. There are no visible waves. The lakes are not frozen, and we know winds blow, because we can see sand dunes created by them. One explanation says the winds die down during Titan's winter season. The cold heavy air must not stir enough even to make small waves. (This means surfing on Titan would only happen in summer. Cowabunga!)

Piercing the thick cloud cover, this radar image of the surface of Titan reveals jagged land formations surrounded by oceans of liquid methane.

Why would humans want to travel to Titan? Three good reasons come to mind.

If there is life on Titan, it would be a natural laboratory for scientists to study how life might evolve on an alien world, how life gets started in the universe, and whether life on Earth and Titan has anything in common.

The second reason is a bit more fun. Have you ever dreamed of flying like a bird? You would be able to experience this here. Talk about really cool X Games! On Titan, the gravity is only 14 percent of what we experience back on Earth. If you weigh 60 pounds on Earth, you would weigh just 9 pounds on Titan. Now picture a set of thin Mylar bird wings, each measuring 3 feet by 7 feet (0.9 m x 2.1 m) strapped on to your arms. Taking a running start, you could lift right off the ground and fly through the air. That's what I'm talking about, Titan!

The last reason has far-reaching possibilities. Titan today is a cold, forbidding distant moon. It has been like this since the solar system formed. Titan won't always be this way. In about five billion years, when our sun swells up into a red giant, it may consume the Earth. This sounds ominous. The good news is that over the next few millions of years, the expanded sun will send out more heat into the farthest regions of our solar system. Titan, the frigid space freezer, will warm up considerably. Responding to these changes in the environment, new life on the surface may emerge. It's possible some of that new life may include migrating human beings arriving in spaceships at their new home. When our sun reaches the last phases of its life, we may jump at the chance to pack up everything and move to Titan!

Billions of years from now, as the expanding red giant sun warms Titan, its freezing methane lakes will evaporate into space, leaving behind temperate oceans of liquid water and possibly life adapted to this new emerging world.

PLUTO & CHARON

STARDATE AUGUST 24, 2006: *Attention members of the solar system! Pluto has been downgraded to a "dwarf" planet! Straighten up and fly right or you could be next! Over and out . . .*

The International Astronomical Union voted to demote Pluto not because of its shape, size, or orbital path as many people believe. As a planet, Pluto is rounder than Saturn and Jupiter. It orbits around the sun just like the rest of the planets in our solar system. Pluto took the fall because of the neighborhood it hangs out in!

Way out beyond Neptune, there exists a region of our solar system called the Kuiper Belt. This is a chilly expanse containing hundreds of thousands of small ice-covered rocks and an estimated trillion or more comets. Located so far away from the sun, these leftovers from the formation of the solar system are poorly illuminated and difficult to see from Earth. Pluto resides in this chaotic region. While many earthlings were upset by its planetary demotion, Pluto stood loud and proud! As space scientists were about to find out, dwarf planets can be unique and fascinating, too.

STARDATE JULY 14, 2015: *Oh, Pluto? Are you ready for your close-up?*

On this historic date, NASA's New Horizons spacecraft successfully completed its Pluto flyby, a mission that took more than nine years to reach distant Pluto! Images beamed back to Earth revealed an odd and stunningly beautiful double planetary system, something astronomers had never seen before. This is why Pluto and its moon Charon are our fifth Wonder of the Solar System.

Clyde Tombaugh in 1928 with a telescope he made.

Pluto was discovered in 1930 by a young assistant astronomer named Clyde Tombaugh at the Lowell Observatory in Arizona; the new planet became a global sensation. A worldwide contest was launched to find a name for Tombaugh's planetary find, which was believed to be about the size of the Earth. Over breakfast with her mother and grandfather, a young British girl interested in Greek and Roman mythology made a suggestion. Venetia Burney thought Pluto, the name of the Roman god of the Underworld, would fit nicely. Everyone agreed, and the new planet now had a name. But let's pause here for a little intrigue: Did Venetia name Pluto after the Roman god . . . or after a newly introduced Disney cartoon character? Turns out, Mickey Mouse's dog was originally named Rover. In 1931, one year after the discovery of Pluto the planet, Rover changed his name to Pluto; it has been that way ever since. Pluto the cartoon dog was named after Pluto the real planet. Case solved!

In early 1996, Pluto was still considered a planet of the outer solar system. Then astronomers began finding more icy objects like Pluto farther out in the Kuiper Belt. A small group speculated that there could be more little Plutos out there than could ever be counted or named (and definitely more than any schoolkid could memorize for a test!). In 2006, scientists from around the world voted that Pluto, along with the scores of not-yet-found icy objects, would form a new category of planets called dwarf planets.

Today, many scientists do not classify Pluto as a singular dwarf planet. It is closely orbited by its giant moon Charon, and this pair behaves more like a double planetary system instead of a planet and satellite. The Pluto-Charon system is the only double planet found in our solar system.

Our moon is one-quarter the size of Earth. Jupiter's four Galilean moons are also very large but till only about 1/27th the size of Jupiter. Pluto's moon Charon is, impressively, one-half the size of Pluto. They were created together out of a gigantic impact with another object during the early formation of our solar system. The collision blasted a big rocky blob off Pluto that eventually cooled into Charon. Just like our moon tugs on Earth's oceans to create tides, the gravity of Charon's short 6.4-day orbit around Pluto tugs on Pluto, causing it to wobble back and forth, pulling it off center. Evidence shows that instead of the planet controlling the orbit of its moon, both Pluto and Charon control each other's orbit. In fact, they may even share some atmospheric gases, too.

Besides BFF Charon, Pluto has four other moons: Nix, Styx, Hydra, and Kerberos. This means Pluto has five more satellites than moonless Mercury and Venus, four more moons than Earth, and three more moons than Mars. Mapping the orbits of Pluto's moons is challenging because they spin differently from any other moon in the solar system. Instead of orbiting Pluto alone, Nix, Styx, Hydra, and Kerberos orbit both Charon and Pluto; they are satellites of both. All these reasons reinforce why Pluto and Charon are considered the first double planetary system in the solar system.

Pluto and Charon closely resemble each other in several other ways, too. Both Charon and Pluto rotate around on their axis once every 6.4 Earth days. Both are similar in structure and composition. Pluto's surface is covered with polar ice caps, rugged mountains, smooth icy plains, flowing glaciers, and large patches of scarlet-colored organic materials that make it the second red planet in our solar system.

Charon's jagged terrain is covered in mountains, canyons, landslides, and surface colors matching Pluto's. Some differences do exist. There's much less ice on Charon's surface, plus the moon has a strikingly long gash measuring 600 miles (966 km), longer and five times deeper than the Grand Canyon on Earth. This gash appears to have formed sometime in the past as the result of surface freezing and the expansion of ice from water hidden underneath the surface of Charon. Pluto is almost a perfect sphere. It doesn't appear to sag or bulge out around its middle like many other planets do. Typically, a planet with great amounts of ice and solid rock would become asymmetrical or egg-shaped over time. This tells us that long ago, Pluto had a warm interior and possibly even oceans on its surface. Didn't expect that from a dwarf planet, did you?

What would it be like to take a stroll on Pluto? If you were standing on this world, 40 times farther away from the sun than Earth is, the sun would still radiate so brightly it could make your eyes water. When you looked out at the daytime sky, the sun would shine brighter than any other star, casting shadows on the ground. (Here's a little experiment that's easy to do: step outside about five minutes after the sun has set, or about five to ten minutes before it rises in the morning, and you'll have a good idea of how bright the sun is during lunch recess on Pluto.)

Since the sun resembles a dazzling white star in the sky, sunsets here would not result in warm colors splashed across the sky. The sun would set on the horizon and blink out. Because Pluto is a smaller planetary body, the curvature on this icy world would easily be seen. No matter where you looked, the curved horizon would be visible 1.25 miles (1.98 km) in any direction.

Here's an interesting situation you don't see on Earth. Sometimes Pluto's atmosphere is present and sometimes it's not. On Earth, this could really cause problems. But it seems to be normal on Pluto. The dwarf planet's unusual orbit is oval as it travels around the sun. At times, Pluto is closer to the sun than Neptune is, at other times it's much farther away than Neptune. At its extreme distance from the sun, Pluto's atmosphere freezes and falls to the ground, covering everything with a delicate frost. As Pluto crosses Neptune's orbit and moves closer to the sun, this frosty top melts and returns as an atmosphere.

CLYDE TOMBAUGH WAS only twenty-four years old when he discovered Pluto on a photographic glass plate on February 18, 1930. Working in the unheated observatory outside Flagstaff, Arizona, in February would have been a teeth-chattering experience. There were no fancy subzero sportswear jackets or electric heated pants to keep him warm. Thick wool coats, heavy gloves, and wool caps pulled down tight were the only protection from the freezing overnight temperatures.

Clyde found employment at the Lowell Observatory because his college plans had been ruined

As Pluto draws closer to the sun, its ephemeral blue atmosphere gently glows along the horizon. Farther away from the sun, the atmosphere will freeze, fall to the ground, and remain as a frosty covering until Pluto orbits nearer to the sun again.

by damaging hailstorms that wiped out the crops on his family farm in Kansas. With his passion for astronomy and building things, he salvaged pieces of wood and parts from old milking machines to make his own telescope. Every night he observed and made drawings of the objects he saw. Just one year after starting to observe the sky, he sent one of his drawings of Mars to the Lowell Observatory for academic review. The reply? "Come to Flagstaff. We'd like to offer you a job as celestial photographer." Tombaugh got out of Kansas faster than a tornado!

His new job sounded glamorous, but indeed it wasn't. The photographic glass plates used as film were big and heavy; the telescope he used was hard to move around in the dark and became so cold in winter that if you touched your tongue to it, your tongue would freeze onto the telescope. That would hurt!

Clyde Tombaugh lived to age ninety. His dying wish was to see what this little planet that had changed his life looked like. He would have been thrilled to know that on July 14, 2015, NASA's New Horizons flew past Pluto with a box of some of his ashes attached to its upper deck. The spacecraft took him on a journey no human had ever traveled before. Pluto presented the most stunning views ever imagined. Jagged dark mountains of rock-hard water ice with nitrogen glaciers flowing around them rotated into view. Two towering volcanoes stood side by side, red-colored terrains pockmarked with craters appeared, and best of all, a gigantic flat plain that mission scientists named Tombaugh Regio (region) faced directly into the spacecraft cameras. Why did they pick this flat plain to honor Tombaugh? It looked like a gigantic heart!

Rocketing past Pluto into deep space, Clyde Tombaugh's ashes will become the first human remains to ever go beyond our solar system. Best of all, his dreams of seeing the face of Pluto came true.

If you sent a text message home via the Pluto network, it would take 4.5 hours to reach your friends due to the great distance through space that emoticons must travel!

PLANET NINE

OUR UNIVERSE IS full of surprises, but nothing equals the cosmic hunt that is happening right now to locate a new, as-yet-unseen giant planet in the outer region of our solar system. Nicknamed Planet Nine, this world is surmised to be about four to five times the size of Earth.

In modern times, the number of planets in our solar system has changed. The English word *planet* derives from the Greek word *planetes*, which means "wanderers." (So next time your little brother or sister wanders off, you can say, "Come back here, you little planet!")

The ancient Greeks considered any object that moved across the sky against the background stars to be a planet, including the sun and moon. (They were grouped together with Mercury, Venus, Mars, Saturn, and Jupiter.) Today we know the sun is a star and the moon is a satellite of Earth, but early observers didn't know this.

All these objects could be followed visually as they traced arcs across the sky. Telescopes and keen mathematics were needed to track down and find Uranus, Neptune, and Pluto. As telescopes became more powerful, astronomers were able to peer farther into the outer regions of our solar neighborhood, resulting in exciting new discoveries. In 2016, scientists announced they had found possible evidence of a behemoth giant planet at the edge

of our solar system. It would be a world so dark and distant, it would be easy to miss. The big question today is, does Planet Nine truly exist? Astronomers are currently using the Subaru telescope in Hawaii to try to find mystery Planet Nine.

IT WAS MARCH 13, 1781. A young British amateur astronomer named William Herschel was in his garden scanning the skies with his homemade telescope when he detected an odd greenish-colored object not seen before. Over the course of a few more evenings, the object seemed to move against the starry background of the night sky. At first Herschel imagined he had discovered a comet. For a young amateur astronomer, this would be thrilling. People who found new comets became famous. Much to his surprise, professional astronomers looking at this new celestial body realized it was not a comet. It was the grandest discovery of all time! William Herschel had found a new planet. Located a considerable distance beyond Saturn, the new planet was named Uranus, after the Greek god of the sky and husband of Mother Earth.

Neptune (aka planet #8 if you're keeping track!) was a bit harder to find. Measuring the orbit of Uranus, French mathematician and astronomer Alexis Bouvard detected that sometimes Uranus slowed down in its orbit and other times sped up during its eighty-four-year trip around the sun. He calculated that something big must be pulling on it from deeper space. A few years later, Bouvard's research led to the simultaneous discovery of Neptune in 1846 by British astronomer John Couch Adams and French astronomer Urbain Le Verrier. Both saw the planet through telescopes at almost the same time from different locations. Its strong cobalt-blue color prompted it to be named after the Roman god of the oceans. However, research was still not complete. Something else now seemed to be pulling on both Uranus and Neptune. Could it possibly be another planet even farther out in space? At the start of the twentieth century, this seemed almost too incredible to be true.

American astronomer Percival Lowell began the search for this mystery planet in 1915 while working at the Lowell Observatory in Arizona. He surveyed the skies extensively for years, but ultimately never located the unknown orb. In 1930, fifteen years after Lowell's passing, Clyde Tombaugh, then an assistant at the Lowell Observatory, made his famous discovery. We know Pluto was named after the Roman god of the Underworld, but its planetary symbol, "PL," was also used to honor Percival Lowell, the first astronomer to search for it.

As we learned earlier, Pluto resides in a thick doughnut-shaped band of small frozen astronomical bodies orbiting beyond Neptune called the Kuiper Belt. Because these objects are so small and far away

KUIPER BELT
ERIS
EARTH
CERES
CHARON
PLUTO
SUN
NEPTUNE
HAUMEA
MAKEMAKE
Charon
Pluto
Ceres
Haumea
Makemake
Eris

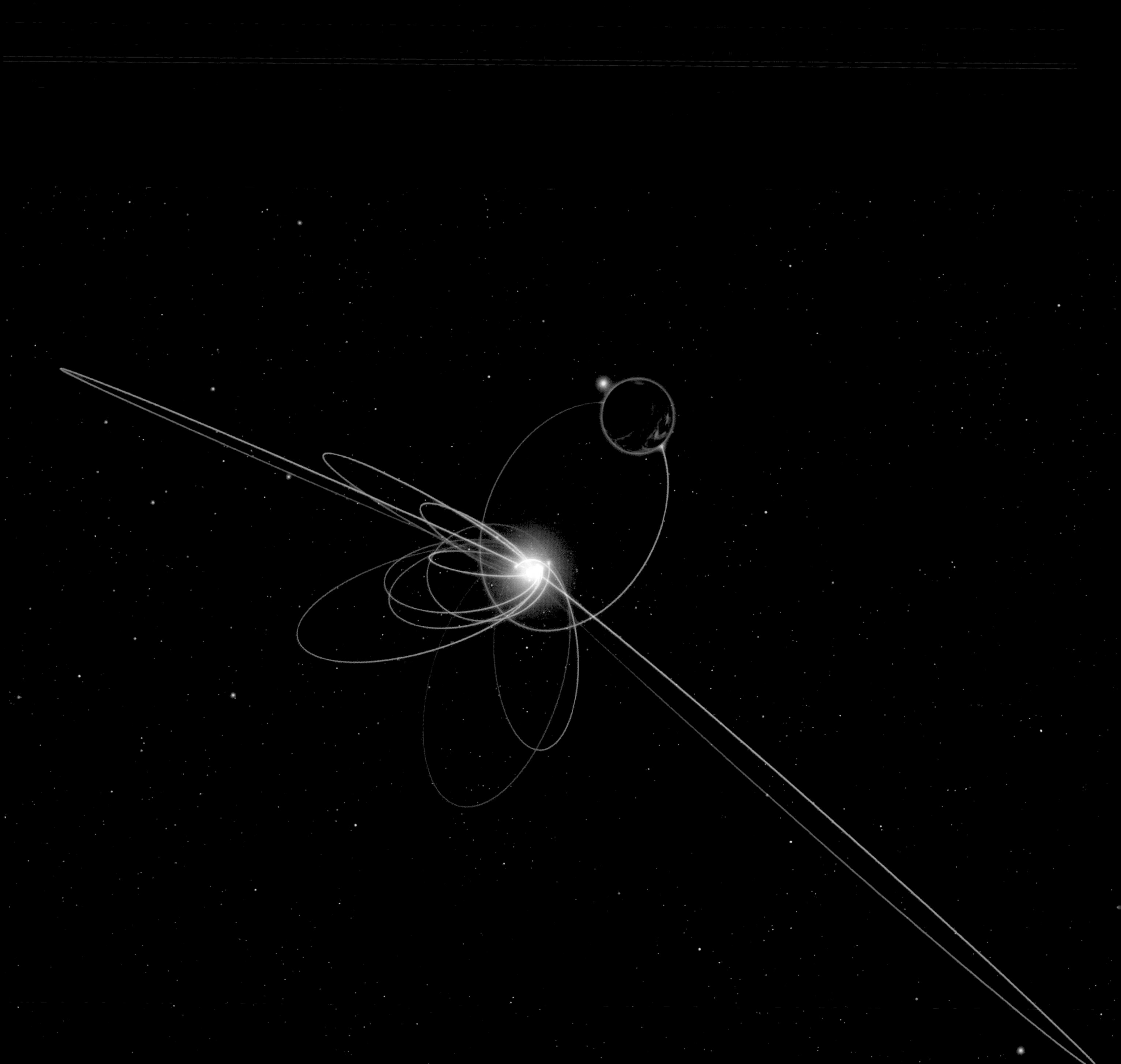

Planet Nine may be a smaller version of the ice giants Uranus and Neptune but about four to five times larger than Earth. One big clue to its existence was the discovery of six Kuiper Belt objects orbiting the same mystery spot in space, as if Planet Nine was pulling on all of them.

from the sun, they are very difficult to see clearly. They look like faint stars in the largest telescopes. Astronomers identify them by taking detailed photographs of the same area of the sky at intervals. They search for star-like objects that have changed positions over time. In 2005, astronomers used this method to locate an object, named Eris, about the same size as Pluto. After much vigorous debate, the astronomers of the world established a new category, dwarf planets, in which to place these small worlds located beyond Neptune. More discoveries quickly followed, adding to the number of dwarf planets, which now included Makemake, Eris, Haumea, and Ceres. Instead of rocky planets like Earth and Mars, these worlds were a combination of one-third rock and two-thirds ice. The search was afoot for even more dwarf planets in the Kuiper Belt when a startling discovery was made. Something in deepest space was changing the orbits of some of the larger Kuiper Belt objects—and that something was really big! Today, NASA scientists are closing in on the trail of this dark world currently referred to as mystery Planet Nine.

Planet Nine won't receive an official name until it is located and identified. Oddly enough, astronomers may have already discovered it, but it hasn't registered with them yet. It's possible that in the photo archives of major observatories, there may be an image with Planet Nine in it.

Some astronomers suspect this mystery planet orbits just beyond the farthest regions of the Kuiper Belt, near the outer boundaries of our solar system. How did they find it? They noticed something odd in an area of the sky they were investigating: six extremely distant Kuiper Belt objects the size of tall buildings kept coming together at the same point in space. The odds of this happening naturally were one in fifteen thousand. The best explanation was that there was a large invisible object controlling their orbits. When calculations came in, the result indicated a massive outer planet might be to blame. This mysterious world appeared to be in a highly elliptical (or oval-shaped) orbit, taking 15,000 to 20,000 years to complete one trip around the sun. There's no need for birthday cake on Planet Nine, unless you plan to live to be at least 15,000 years old!

How long would a voyage to Planet Nine take? This is something of a tricky question because we know that Planet Nine's orbit is not round. Traveling at the highest rocket speeds possible, it would take approximately 60 years to reach our destination when it is at its closest approach to the sun, or 355 years when it is at the farthest point away in its orbit. Who has that much time?

Crazy cold temperatures can be expected on Planet Nine. Surrounding it may be a slushy atmosphere like the one on Neptune. Or it may not have any atmosphere at all. Either way the average daytime temperature would be a bone-chilling -423 degrees F (-253 degrees C) below zero, colder than any temperatures found on Earth.

Located in the constellation Cetus the Whale, hints of Planet Nine were detected at a distance of six hundred times farther away than the Earth is from the sun. Talk about cosmic isolation! Planet Nine is fifteen times farther away from Earth than Pluto is, and we all know Pluto is way, way out there! Let's not forget it took NASA's New Horizons spacecraft nine and a half years to reach that dwarf planet.

Where did this mystery planet come from? Planet Nine may have formed at the same time as the rest of the solar system some 4.5 billion years ago. Was there enough rock and ice to make such a large planet so far away from the sun? We don't know the answer to that just yet.

A different hypothesis is known as the "heist scenario." This idea suggests that our own sun is a galactic thief! Planet Nine may have been a rogue world thrown out of another solar system. As it was drifting alone through space, our sun may have "lifted it" as it was passing by.

Could this solar heist affect us in any way? Some suspect Planet Nine's long slow orbit around the sun could trigger periodic bombardments of Earth by comets. Passing through the Kuiper Belt, the breeding ground of comets, Planet Nine could easily dislodge large swarms, pushing them in toward the sun. Some of those displaced comets might even hit the Earth! Astronomers are continuing their search in the region where they suspect Planet Nine may be located. Right now Planet Nine is just a hypothesis that demonstrates how science works. Tantalizing new information eventually leads to future discoveries. Space science teams are collaborating around the world, sharing new ideas and information. As they work together, another window to the universe may open for all to share. The discovery of a new planet is a once-in-a-lifetime event. It shows how the quest for knowledge can radically change our views of the solar system and beyond. How soon may we welcome Planet Nine into our solar neighborhood? Only time will tell.

Although Earth has never been hit by multiple comets before, other objects in our solar system may have. Disrupted comets at the edge of the solar system could collide with our planet.

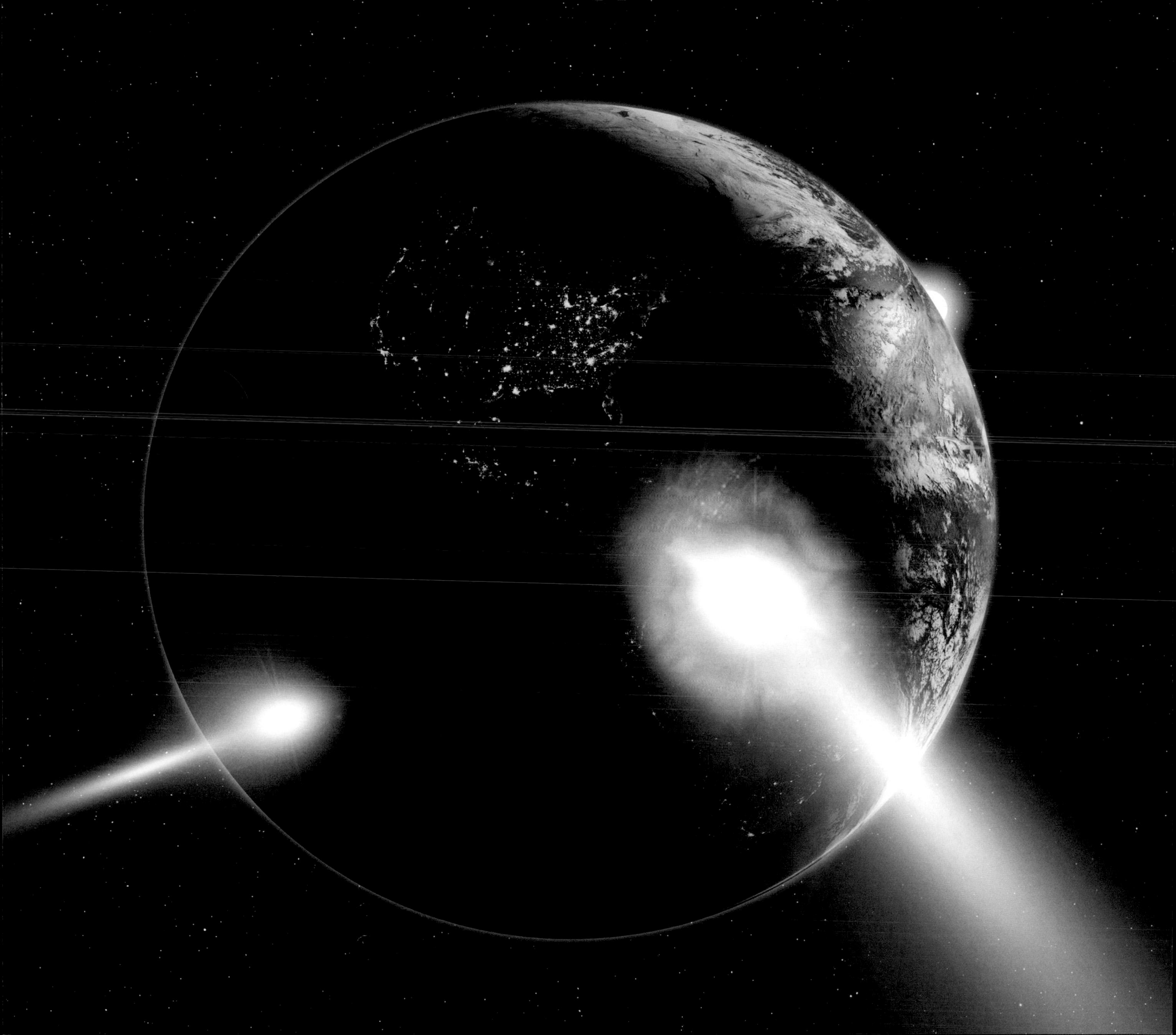

EARTH & MOON

MEXICO'S AZTEC CIVILIZATION called it *Tonantzin*, meaning "our mother." The ancient Greeks named it *Gaia*, the Chinese *Hou Tau*, and the Hindus *Bhuma Devi*. All of these translate into the loving title of "goddess of the land." More than a thousand years ago, Germanic tribes named Anglo-Saxons inhabiting Great Britain called their world *Erda,* meaning "ground" or "soil." By the Middle Ages, besides discussing jousting matches and maidens in distress, people referred to their planet as *Erthe*. The English translation of this word is "Earth," the name many of us recognize as our home planet today.

Had our ancestors known more, they might have called it "The Right Planet." In our solar system, Earth is the right size for harboring life. It has the right amount of gravity to keep its atmosphere from floating away. Earth orbits the right type of star for life to begin and evolve over long periods of time. Spinning around on its axis once every 24 hours, Earth has the right-size moon to stabilize it so it doesn't wobble around

The habitable or green zone around a star is where water exists as a gas, as a liquid, and as ice.

creating disastrous winds and tides. Earth orbits in the "Goldilocks zone" or just the right distance from its star. It isn't too close to the sun and hot like Venus, or too far away and frigid like Mars. Located in this right zone, water can exist as a liquid, a gas, or a solid, all at the same time. On this right type of world, water is a critical element for the emergence of life . . . like us!

It may have never crossed your mind that a planet's size can determine whether it can host life. On smaller worlds like Mars, weaker gravity lets the atmosphere drift away into space. That's not good news. Planets with four to five times the mass of Earth can't form into rocky planets anymore. Instead, they become frozen ice giants like Uranus and Neptune. Back on Earth, the gravitational field generated by our world fits our bodies perfectly. If you were to take a stroll on the moon, you'd experience being just one-sixth of your normal weight. In space, we float midair because our bodies weigh nothing in zero gravity. But the human body does not respond well to zero gravity. On the other end of the spectrum, we'd weigh much more on the outer planets of our solar system, like Jupiter and Saturn. However, we would not be able to stand on the surfaces of these two worlds without being crushed by the extreme atmospheric pressure of these gas giants pushing down on top of us.

When someone buys a house, they always look for a good location. Nobody wants to build their house two hundred feet underwater, or perched on a big boulder hanging over the edge of a cliff. Our Earth is situated 93 million miles (150 million km) away from the sun, in a location called the habitable zone, where temperatures are moderate and water remains liquid. As we discovered on Europa, water is the best solvent for transporting necessary vitamins, minerals, and gases inside living cells and

Forged from an earlier collision, our moon formed from rings of debris that once surrounded Earth.

organisms. Fortunately for us, water is abundant on Earth. Nearly three-quarters of our planet is covered with it. Earth also orbits a very stable star that does not send out massive flares of radiation like other stars do. Our sun has a projected lifetime of about 10 billion years. Our time on this planet has been short relative to the sun's long lifespan, and there appears to be ample time for new forms of life to evolve on our world and call it home. So we might say, "Sit back and enjoy the show!"

Now let's consider the life-maintaining relationship between the Earth and our moon. Born out of a cosmic collision during the early formation of our solar system, the moon stabilizes the Earth's dizzying spin at 24,000 miles (40,000 km) per hour. If the moon disappeared, our planet would wobble like a spinning top, causing polar ice to move from the poles to the equator and then back again. Without the gravitational tug-of-war between the Earth and the moon, the rotation of the Earth would be much faster. How fast could it be? One day on our world would only be six hours long. This means there would be more than one thousand days in a year! All these factors combine to demonstrate just how simple laws of physics can influence a planet like Earth. It reinforces just how special our world is.

Just a three-day journey by spaceship away from home, the moon has been our constant companion for billions of years, orbiting Earth like a moth around a porch light. Would anything happen to Earth if we changed this relationship just a tiny bit? What if the moon orbited Earth in the opposite direction? This is called retrograde motion, and two-thirds of all moons in our solar system orbit their planets in this opposite direction. To occupy this type of orbit, the moon would have been captured instead of being formed out of a collision like it actually was. With no planetary smash-up, there would be no tilt to the Earth's axis. Without any tilt, say good-bye to summer, fall, winter, and spring. The seasons would never change. With Earth's equator bathed in constant summer sunlight, temperatures would soar. More ocean water would evaporate, forming massive rain clouds, creating more hurricanes and tornadoes. With the moon orbiting in the opposite direction from the Earth's rotation, there would be more gravitational drag between the two. This increased pull would eventually send the moon slowly spiraling in toward us, speeding up its orbit as it drew nearer. Over millions of years, the moon would grow larger in our sky, shining brighter at night as it zipped across the sky. Ocean tides would be more extreme, changing from high tides to low tides much faster. Eventually, the moon would pile into the Earth, clearing our world of life. This would not be pretty! Planet Earth would become a very different world . . . a place we might not recognize as home.

UNLIKE MARS OR the moon, planet Earth has witnessed many changes to its climate, landscapes, and life. Ours is an ever-evolving world. If we time-traveled back two billion years, we'd find Earth covered in vast oceans tinted red by the single-celled plants living in them. Jumping back just 75 million years, Earth would

TWO BILLION YEARS AGO

75 MILLION YEARS AGO

15,000 YEARS AGO

be teeming with dinosaurs and gigantic pterodactyls soaring overhead. Jungles and swamps would cover the planet, and for us it would be uncomfortably warm and steamy. Fifteen thousand years ago, Earth would be layered in sheets of ice from the last ice age. Hairy ancestors of elephants called mastodons would roam across snowy fields searching for food. Today, in what we call the modern age, the glaciers, ice, and snow have retreated back to the polar regions. Gone are the mastodons and saber-toothed tigers that thrived during the ice age. Human beings, or to use the scientific term, *Homo sapiens*, now dominate the landscape. We rule planet Earth! But heads up: Earth will not always look the way it does right now. Time now to peer into the future: In a few billion years, the sun will grow hot enough to boil away the Earth's oceans. Once again, our planet will change. It is all part of the natural cycles of life and climate on Tonantzin, or Mother Earth.

Of all the wonders of the solar system, Earth is the only place we are certain hosts life. There are scores of types of bacteria and single-celled plants and ani-

PRESENT DAY

FOUR BILLION YEARS FROM NOW

mals living miles beneath the surface that never see the light of day or ever feel rain. Earth's oceans are rich with life, but so are its continents, mountain ranges, deserts, polar regions, and even regions in the clouds. Virtually from the start, life has been a part of our planet. Precisely how life began is still a mystery. We simply do not know how or why different chemicals and molecules joined together to become aware of their surroundings, take in food or sunlight for energy, and begin reproducing. Is the formation of life something that naturally happens throughout the universe, or has life only occurred here on this blue gem called Earth? Are there other Earth-like planets out among the stars awaiting our discovery? What might those worlds look like and what might be living on them? For now, Earth and all of its inhabitants remain the exception among all the other planets and moons in our solar neighborhood and possibly beyond. Earth truly is the Seventh Wonder of the Solar System . . . and possibly the universe.

"Whatever else astronomy may or may not be, who can doubt it to be the most beautiful of all the sciences?"

—Isaac Asimov

INTO THE FUTURE

PRIVATE SPACE TRAVEL or "space tourism" for non-astronauts like us is quickly becoming a reality. One private American company hopes to take tourists to the moon by 2020, and another company anticipates expeditions to Mars beginning as soon as 2030. Though it is high risk, many people are seeking the "final frontier" called outer space.

On our imaginary journey through the vast realms of our solar system, we marveled at wonders found nowhere else. Our planetary voyage took us past monstrous volcanoes, sparkling icy rings, and vast hidden oceans. We walked on an orange-tinted moon that may support primordial forms of life. We stood on the only double planet in our solar system and had a glimpse into how the scientific method works as we narrow the search for mysterious Planet Nine. Most importantly, we have taken a closer look at Earth, the only home any of us have . . . so far.

Our world stands apart from everything else in our solar system. Critical for human existence, Earth remains a small fragile planet. Taking the best possible care of our world ensures our own survival. Outer space is a big and lonely place. Unimaginable distances exist between the stars, making travel between them staggering to think about. But the day will come when we will be capable of exploring far beyond our own solar 'hood. Is this our power and destiny as a species? First, we construct extraordinary wonders here on Earth out of metal and stone. Then, we build magnificent spaceships and robotic explorers that extend our reach to the Seven Wonders of the Solar System. As dazzling as these may be, you might ask, what surprises await us farther out there among the stars? What do the Seven Wonders of the Universe look like? Well now, that's another story . . .

OTHER WONDERS

WHILE RESEARCHING THIS BOOK, I was interested to learn that the Seven Wonders of the Ancient World were a bit controversial. At the time they existed, there was no single agreed-upon list. Greek writers and travelers promoted their own favorite sites over others. Some people felt the Egyptian Labyrinth, a vast temple divided into twelve great courts by winding walls, surpassed the Great Pyramid of Giza. Many thought it should have been included on the wonders list. Others replaced the Lighthouse at Alexandria with the Walls of Babylon. Over many centuries, one list finally emerged and that's the one we recognize today. Narrowing down the Seven Wonders of the Solar System was no easier.

Some might say the Great Red Spot on Jupiter, a huge cyclonic color-changing hurricane that has raged on for at least the past 400 years, should be included. Others might vote for the ice volcanoes of Saturn's moon Enceladus. Why weren't the great cliffs of Uranus's moon Miranda included? How could the volcanoes of Io be missing? What about the football-shaped tumbling dwarf planet Haumea, or the Grand Canyon of Mars, Valles Marineris? Why isn't dwarf planet Ceres in there? All these wonderful possibilities were carefully considered. My selections became clear after asking myself this simple question: If I had a spaceship, and I could send back selfies from seven astounding places in our solar system, where would they be? The answers soon became clear. All the other magnificent wonders mentioned above would have to be visited on future trips.

Bottom (left): ice volcanoes of Enceladus; center (left to right): dwarf planet Ceres, Jupiter's Great Red Spot, egg-shaped dwarf planet Haumea; top (right): canyons of Mars.

DREAMS OF OUTER SPACE

GROWING UP, I was attracted to anything that had to do with outer space. I had a lunch box with astronauts pictured on the side. In my bedroom I built models of rockets, spaceships, and space stations. I read books about space travel and science fiction and looked at the moon through my trusty three-inch reflecting telescope. Peering at the lunar craters and mountains made me feel as if I were almost there.

As a young person, the one thing that truly inspired me the most was the pioneering work of Chesley Bonestell, now considered the father of space art. I was hooked by his paintings of the future exploration of the moon and the solar system. His illustrations portrayed outer space as big, dark, and distant, with so many beautiful places for earthlings to visit. The very thought of it made my mind and imagination soar to new heights.

Even then I realized the stars, located light-years away, were too distant for humans to ever reach. The solar system was our celestial playground, our classroom to learn more about the Earth and our place in the universe. As a certifiable grade-school space dreamer, I accepted that even if I never walked on the surface of the moon, I still wanted to study space and explore it through my studies. Outer space would always remain a big part of my life. And luckily for me, it became my career as an artist, writer, and astronomer! Even though I have a large observatory at my home located high in the Rocky Mountains, I still get a thrill looking through my little three-inch reflecting telescope at the phases of Venus, the stripes on Jupiter, and the gorgeous rings of Saturn! All this has taught me a valuable lesson. The things you love to do today may someday turn out to be what you do for the rest of your life. How wonderful is that?

IN THE STUDIO WITH DAVID A. AGUILAR

WHAT A CHALLENGE building a replica of the largest volcano in the solar system out of plaster of Paris! I know, you may be thinking, why build Olympus Mons? The only images scientists have of this monster volcano were taken from spacecraft in orbit around Mars; the perspective is looking straight down at it. So far, no Mars rover has ever been able to image the mountain from the ground. So I built a tabletop model to use in my artwork.

Before I began, I had to do a little math to determine just how large I could make my model and what its proportions should be. The real Olympus Mons is 374 miles (624 km) in diameter, about the size of Arizona, and 16 miles (25 km) high—I would definitely have to go *scale* model. If I made my replica 22 inches (56 cm) in diameter, the summit would be about about 1 inch (25 mm) high with about a 3-inch wide (75 mm) caldera, or opening at the top from which the lava flowed out. Now the project seemed more manageable!

Here is how you can build a model of Olympus Mons. The materials are simple, inexpensive, and easy to find:

- One 30-inch square sheet of 1-inch-thick white rigid insulation foam board. You can get this at a building supply store and cut it down to size using a kitchen bread knife with the help of an adult.
- One 25-pound bag of plaster of Paris (same store, in the aisle with the wall plastering supplies)
- A roll of inexpensive paper towels
- One old newspaper
- Black felt-tip pen to trace the volcano outline on the foam board
- Pencil, toothpicks, and wooden coffee stirrers; you'll use these as tools for adding detail around the edges of your wet plaster model.
- Recycled yogurt containers for mixing the paint wash
- Acrylic paints to color the finished volcano (I used red, black, yellow, and white mixed together.)
- One small plastic bucket for mixing the plaster of Paris with water
- Small hot glue gun

- Inexpensive 2-inch-wide paintbrush
- Old clothes in case you get plaster of Paris on them
- And imagination, of course!

To get started, go online and download a NASA image of Olympus Mons. Here are two options:

photojournal.jpl.nasa.gov/catalog/PIA00300

en.wikipedia.org/wiki/Olympus_Mons#/media/File:Olympus_Mons_alt.jpg

Use a copy machine or desktop printer to create an enlarged print. This gives you the proper dimensions you'll need for tracing.

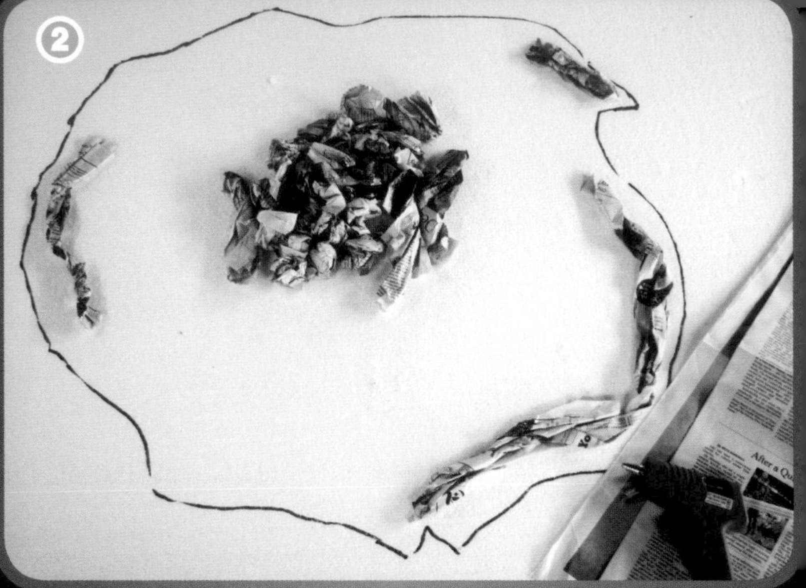

1. Cut out your enlarged copy. Trace it on the foam board.

2. Next, tear out small pieces of newspaper and roll them into small 1-inch-diameter (25 mm) balls. Using the hot glue gun, attach the newspaper balls onto the center and wadded-up newspaper to the edges. So far so good!

Pour about two cups of cold water into a plastic bucket (hot water makes plaster of Paris set too quickly). Fill a paper cup with the dry plaster and start sprinkling it into the water without stirring. I let the sifted plaster build up until the plaster absorbs most of the water. After one cup of plaster has been added, then you can stir it with a wooden spoon or a stick. Add more water or plaster until the plaster resembles thin pancake batter. It is now ready to be applied.

3. Dip torn sheets of paper towels into the plaster mixture and then lay them down on top of the balled-up newspapers. Add more plaster towel pieces until you reach the edges of the volcano printout. Smooth everything down using wet fingers. Keep adding layers until the plaster begins to set or harden. At this point, stop! Take your coffee stirrer tool and begin to sculpt the edges of the cliffs. Move quickly as the plaster really begins to harden.

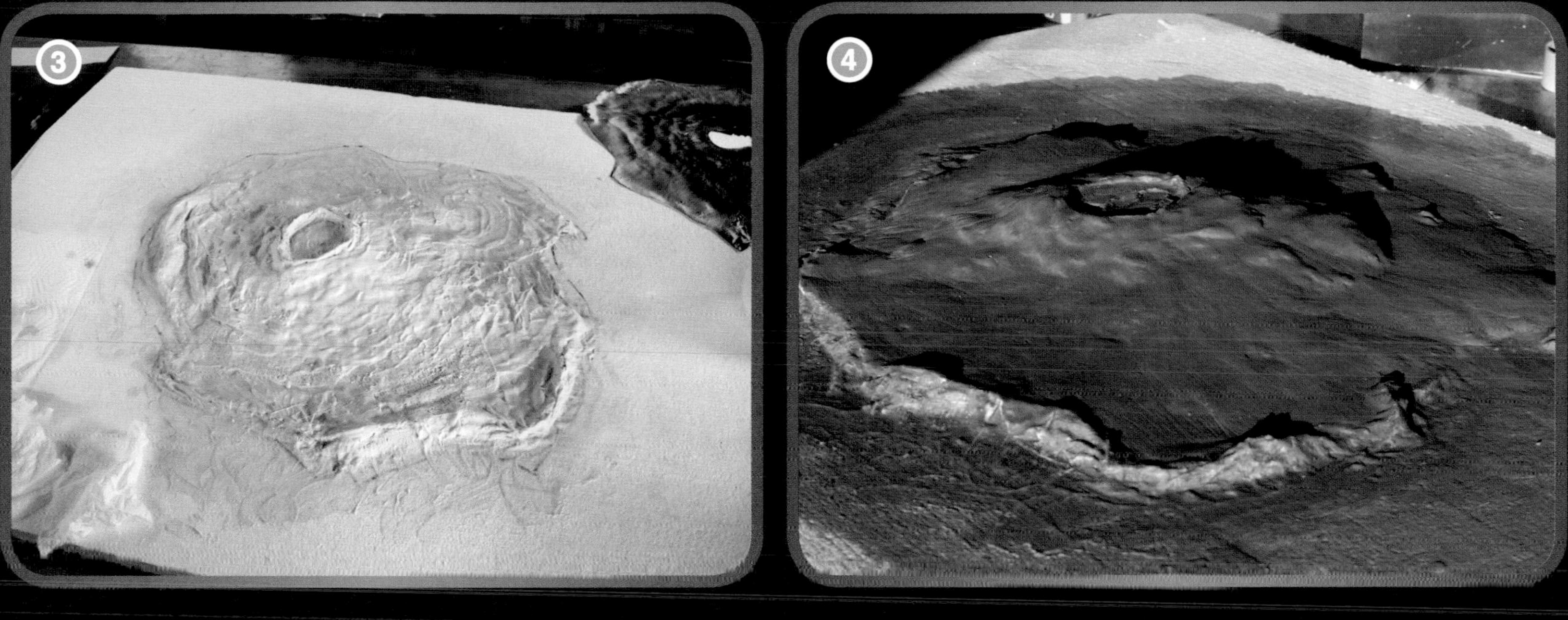

Examine your model. Does it need more plaster built up in certain areas? If so, mix a new batch of plaster of Paris. Smooth it on with your hands. Remember, Olympus Mons has gentle rolling slopes. Only the cliffs are rough and jagged. Work and add more plaster until you are satisfied with the shape of your volcano. The last area to sculpt is the caldera, or the opening on top where the lava originally flowed.

Let your Martian volcano dry overnight.

4 Pour about two inches of cold tap water into an empty plastic container. Add a blob of red and a little black acrylic paint until you have the Martian red color fairly matched to what's shown in this book. Add a little yellow or white to warm it up. Take this wash and paint it over your model with the 2-inch-wide paintbrush. Add more color washes to build up the color. Use a dry brush (dip it into paint and squeeze it with a paper towel to remove most of the paint) with just a little darker red-brown paint on it to highlight the cliff edges around the base. There it is! You now have your own model of Olympus Mons!

KEEP EXPLORING!

BOOKS

Aguilar, David A. *13 Planets: The Latest View of the Solar System and Beyond*. Washington, DC: National Geographic, 2011.

——. *Alien Worlds: Your Guide to Extraterrestrial Life*. Washington, DC: National Geographic, 2013.

——. *Cosmic Catastrophes: Seven Ways to Destroy a Planet Like Earth*. New York: Viking/Smithsonian, 2016.

——. *Space Encyclopedia: A Tour of Our Solar System and Beyond*. Washington, DC: National Geographic, 2013.

——. *Super Stars: The Biggest, Hottest, Brightest, Most Explosive Stars in the Milky Way*. Washington, DC: National Geographic, 2010.

Jennings, Ken. *Junior Genius Guides: Outer Space*. New York: Little Simon, 2015.

Miller, Ron, and Frederick C. Durant III. *The Art of Chesley Bonestell*. New York: Paper Tiger, 2001.

Morgan, Ben, ed. *Space! The Universe as You've Never Seen It Before*. New York: DK Publishing/Smithsonian, 2015.

MEDIA

"NASA's Unexplained Files," Science Channel

www.sciencechannel.com/tv-shows/nasas-unexplained-files

"Space," Smithsonian Channel

www.smithsonianchannel.com/search?q=space

"The Universe," featuring author David A. Aguilar, The History Channel

www.youtube.com/watch?v=0gmdYoI_zGo

WEBSITES

David A. Aguilar author site

davidaguilar.org

NASA/Astronomy Picture of the Day (APOD)

apod.nasa.gov/apod/astropix.html

NASA Cassini Mission to Saturn

nasa.gov/mission_pages/cassini/main/index.html

NASA New Horizons Pluto Mission

pluto.jhuapl.edu/

Smithsonian National Air and Space Museum

nasm.si.edu

Index

Note: Page numbers in *italics* refer to illustrations.

Adams, John Couch, 54
astrology, 9
astronomy, 9–10

Bouvard, Alexis, 54

Charon, 45, 46, 47

double-planetary systems, 46, 47
dwarf planets, *9*, 45, 46, 57. *See also* Pluto

Earth, *8*, 59–67
  atmosphere of, 38
  distance from sun, 62
  formation of, 6, 33
  gravity on, 62
  life on, 61–62, *62*, 64, *66*, 66–67, *67*
  moon of, 46, 61–62, 63, *63*, 64
  orbit of, 61, 62
  rotation of, 63
  water on, 21, 23, 24, *24*, 29, 62–63
Europa, 20–27, *22*
  and conditions for life, 23, 25, *25*
  gravity on, 27
  surface of, 24, 25, *26*, 27
  water on, 23–25, *24*, 27

Galilei, Galileo, 23, *32*, 33
gas giants, *8–9*, 30, 33

Herschel, William, 54
Huygens, Christiaan, 33

ice giants, *9*, 33, 62

Jupiter, *8*
  characteristics of, 8, 29
  formation of, 6, 30
  moons of, *22*, 23–24, 27, 46–47
  radiation belts surrounding, 27
  rings of, 34

Kuiper Belt, 45, 46, 54, 57, 58

Le Verrier, Urbain, 54
Lowell, Percival, 54
Lowell Observatory, 46, 51, 54

Mars, *8*, 12–19
  atmosphere of, 13, 19, 62
  color of, 13, *14*
  formation of, 6, 33
  human exploration of, 18–19
  surface of, 29
  volcanoes of, *14*, 15–18, 19
  water on, 13, 17, 18, 20
Mercury, 6, *8*, 33

Neptune, 6, *9*, 30, 34, 54

Planet Nine, *9*, 52–58
  atmosphere of, 57–58
  clues to existence of, *56*, 57
  distance from sun, 58
  formation of, 58
  search for, 52, 54, 58
Pluto, *9*, 44–51
  atmosphere of, 48, *48–49*
  discovery of, 46, 48, 51, 54
  as double-planetary system, 46, 47
  as dwarf planet, 45
  moons of, 47
  rotation of, 47
  and Tombaugh, 46, 48, 51

robotic probes, 10, *11*, 33–34

Saturn, 6, *9*, 29–30, *31*, 34
Saturn's rings, 28–35
  discovery of, *32*, 33
  and robotic probes, 33–34
  sections of, 30, *30*
  size of, 33, 34
Seven Wonders of the Ancient World, 4, 70
solar system
  birth of, 6, *7*
  habitable zone of, *62*, 62
  planets of, *8–9*
space travel, 69
sun, 6, *7*, *8*, 8

Titan, 36–43
  atmosphere of, 37, 38, 41
  human exploration of, 43
  potential for life on, 38–39, 41, 43
  rotation of, 37–38
  water on, 41, *42–43*
Tombaugh, Clyde, *46*, 46, 48, 51, 54

Uranus, 6, *9*, 30, 34, 54

Venus, *8*
  characteristics of, 8
  formation of, 6, 33
  light reflected from, 29
  orbit of, 9
  temperatures on, 18
  water on, 21

water and life, 21, 23